American Symbols

The Lincoln Memorial

by Mary Firestone

illustrated by Matthew Skeens

PICTURE WINDOW BOOKS
Minneapolis, Minnesota

Special thanks to our advisers for their expertise:

Melodie Andrews, Ph.D., Associate Professor of Early American History
Minnesota State University, Mankato

Terry Flaherty, Ph.D., Professor of English
Minnesota State University, Mankato

Editor: Shelly Lyons
Designers: Abbey Fitzgerald, Amy Muehlenhardt, and Tracy Davies
Page Production: Melissa Kes
Art Director: Nathan Gassman
Associate Managing Editor: Christianne Jones
The illustrations in this book were created digitally.
Photo Credit: Jeremy R. Smith/Shutterstock, 23

Picture Window Books
5115 Excelsior Boulevard, Suite 232
Minneapolis, MN 55416
877-845-8392
www.picturewindowbooks.com

All books published by Picture Window Books
are manufactured with paper containing at least
10 percent post-consumer waste.

Library of Congress Cataloging-in-Publication Data
Firestone, Mary.
The Lincoln Memorial / by Mary Firestone ; illustrated by Matthew Skeens.
p. cm. — (American symbols)
Includes index.
ISBN-13: 978-1-4048-3718-8 (library binding)
ISBN-10: 1-4048-3718-3 (library binding)
1. Lincoln Memorial (Washington, D.C.)—Juvenile literature. 2. Lincoln, Abraham, 1809–1865—
Monuments—Washington (D.C.)—Juvenile literature. 3. Washington (D.C.)—Buildings, structures,
etc.—Juvenile literature. I. Skeens, Matthew. II. Title.
F203.4.L73F57 2008
975.3—dc22   2007004586

Table of Contents

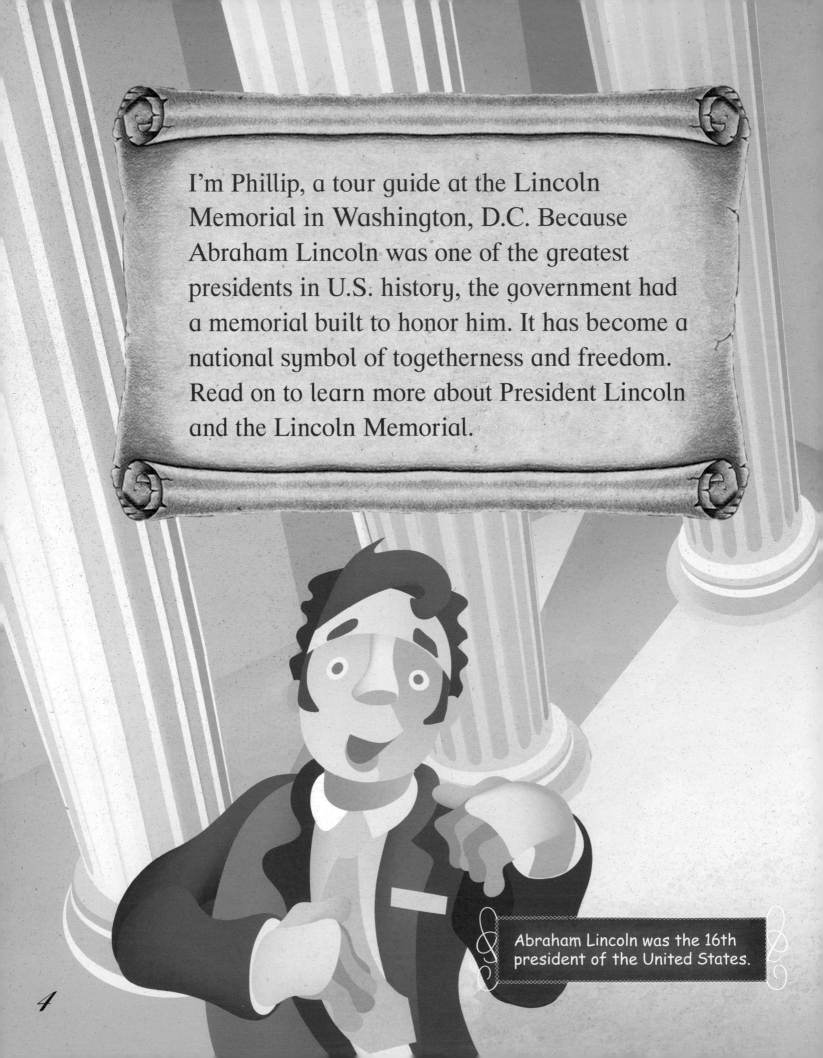

I'm Phillip, a tour guide at the Lincoln Memorial in Washington, D.C. Because Abraham Lincoln was one of the greatest presidents in U.S. history, the government had a memorial built to honor him. It has become a national symbol of togetherness and freedom. Read on to learn more about President Lincoln and the Lincoln Memorial.

Abraham Lincoln was the 16th president of the United States.

4

President Lincoln

Abraham Lincoln led the United States through the Civil War (1861–1865). At the start of the war, some states tried to break away from the United States. Lincoln's army fought to hold the country together. Lincoln also believed slaves should be free. He once said, "If slavery isn't wrong, then nothing is wrong." Lincoln succeeded in winning the Civil War, and the slaves were freed.

Lincoln Is Shot

President Lincoln was shot in 1865 while watching a play at Ford's Theater in Washington, D.C. He died from his wounds. Lincoln's death was a terrible blow to the country. After his death, Americans began talking about a memorial to honor him and his great deeds.

A Swampy Site

Years later, Americans took action to honor President Lincoln. In 1911, Congress formed the Lincoln Memorial Commission. Its job was to pick a location for the memorial and find an architect to design it. Henry Bacon was the architect chosen for the job.

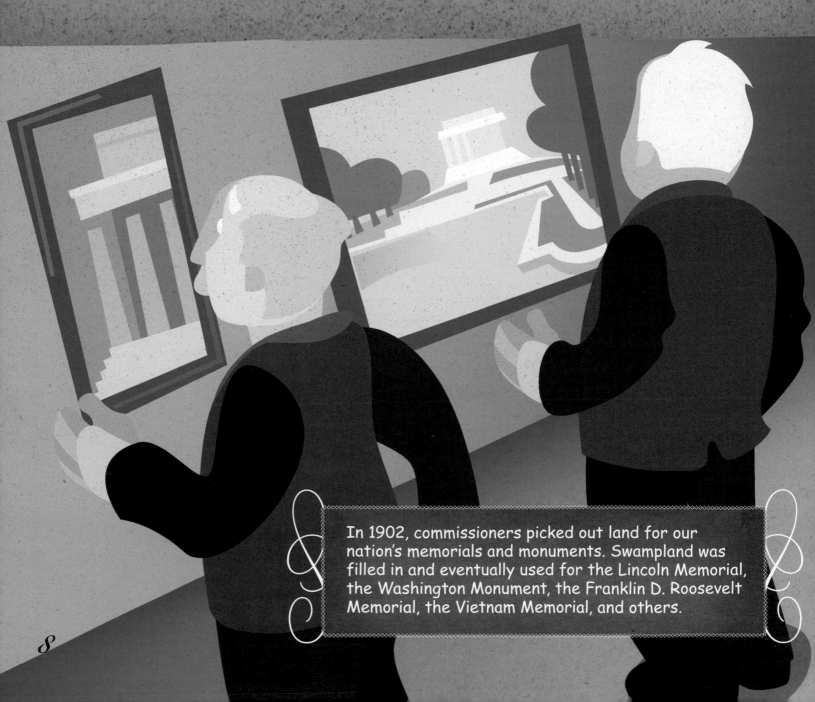

In 1902, commissioners picked out land for our nation's memorials and monuments. Swampland was filled in and eventually used for the Lincoln Memorial, the Washington Monument, the Franklin D. Roosevelt Memorial, the Vietnam Memorial, and others.

The commissioners chose Potomac Park in Washington, D.C., for the memorial. The park was a wet, marshy area. Because of all the water, workers had to build a strong platform for the building.

The Platform

The Lincoln Memorial platform is 14 feet (4.3 meters) high, 257 feet (78.4 m) long, and 187 feet (57 m) wide. Workers spent a full year working on the platform before starting construction on the memorial building.

Work on the Lincoln Memorial began on February 12, 1914. That date would have been Lincoln's 105th birthday.

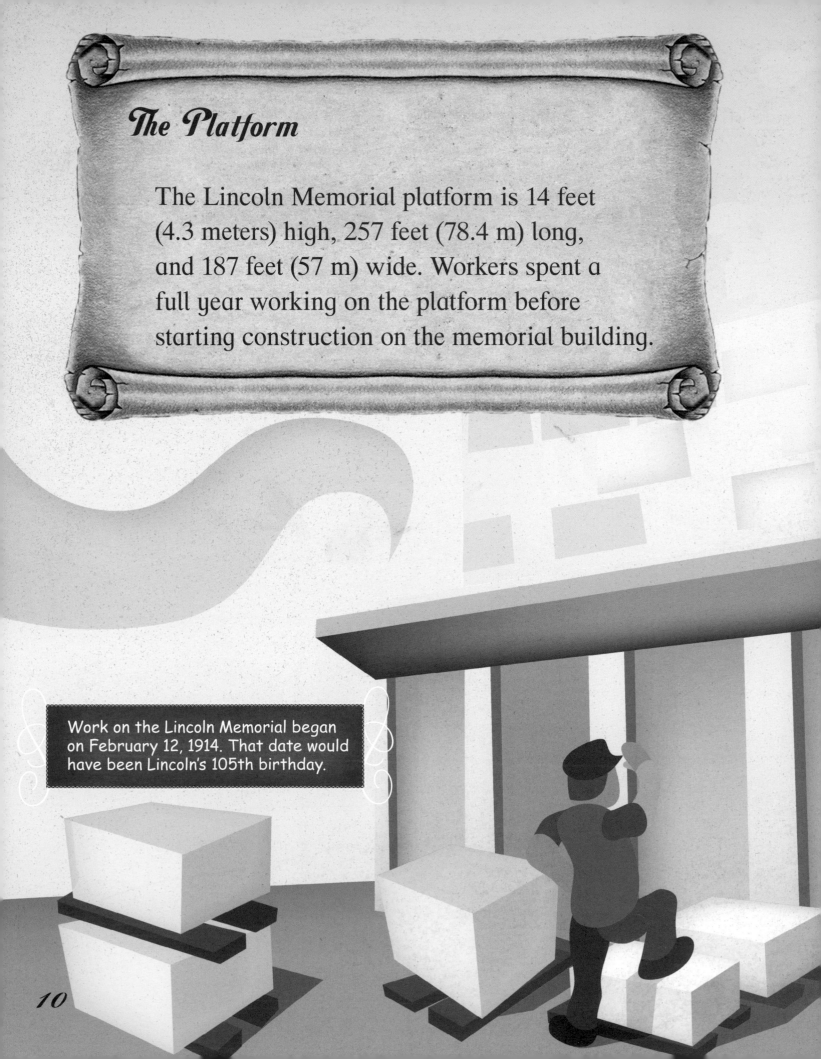

The Building

The Lincoln Memorial is made of different types of U.S. marble. It has 36 columns. These columns stand for the number of states that were part of the United States at the time President Lincoln died.

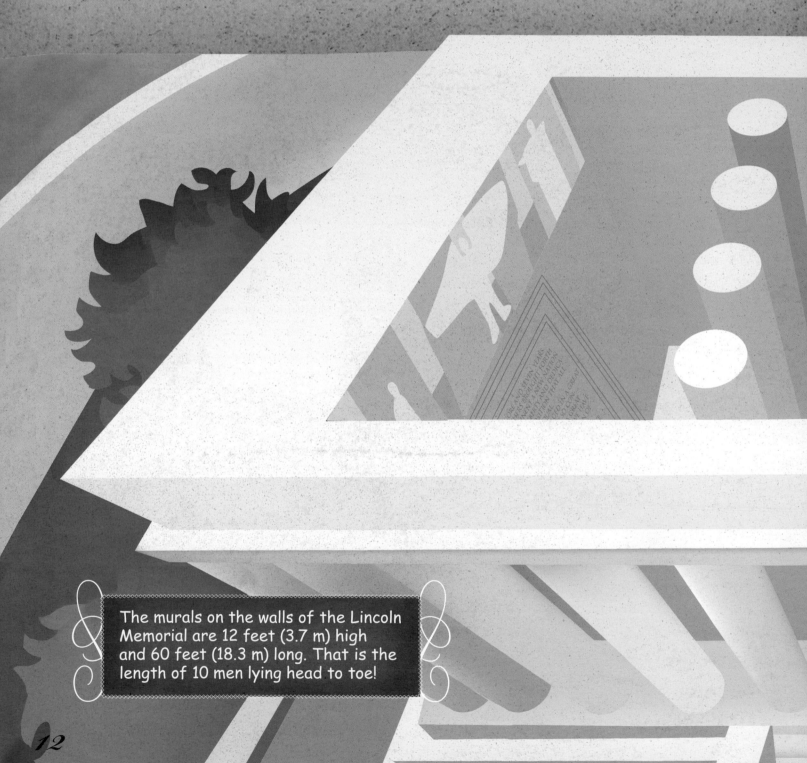

The murals on the walls of the Lincoln Memorial are 12 feet (3.7 m) high and 60 feet (18.3 m) long. That is the length of 10 men lying head to toe!

The memorial is a very large building, but it has only three sections. The center section has a large statue of Abraham Lincoln. The other two sections have walls on which Lincoln's famous speeches were carved by artist Ernest Bairstow. Above the speeches are murals that were painted by Jules Guerin.

The statue of Lincoln is almost as tall as two basketball hoops stacked on top of each other. The statue's head is the size of an armchair. Each thumb is the size of a toaster.

A Huge Statue

An artist named Daniel Chester French designed the Lincoln statue. French was an American who had studied art in Italy. He first planned to make a statue that was only 10 feet (3.1 m) tall. After meeting with Henry Bacon, the two decided the statue needed to be 19 feet (5.8 m) tall.

Putting It Together

Although Daniel French designed the statue of Lincoln, he hired Attilio and Furio Piccirilli to carve it. The brothers came from a famous stone-carving family. First, they cut the white marble into 28 pieces. The brothers then went to work carving the statue from the marble pieces. In the end, the statue was put together like a puzzle.

The Lincoln Memorial is made of marble from different states. The floor is made of pink Tennessee marble, and the statue is made of white Georgia marble. The ceiling is made of Alabama marble.

17

The Dedication

The Lincoln Memorial was finally finished in 1922. A dedication ceremony was held on May 30, 1922. A crowd of more than 50,000 people attended the ceremony. The front row was made up of veterans of the Civil War. Lincoln's son Robert Todd Lincoln was also at the ceremony.

Warren Harding, the 29th president of the United States, led the dedication ceremony of the Lincoln Memorial.

A Place for History

Many important events have taken place at the Lincoln Memorial. People have gathered there to hear speeches and singers. They have also gone there to speak out against war and unfairness.

In 1963, Martin Luther King Jr. gave his famous "I Have a Dream" speech on the memorial steps. He called for Americans of all colors to live together in peace.

Marian Anderson, a famous African-American singer, sang at the Lincoln Memorial in 1939. A crowd of 75,000 people showed up for the concert. After Marian sang the last note, the crowd roared its approval and cheered for more.

You can visit the Lincoln Memorial in Washington, D.C. Millions of tourists come to see this American symbol of togetherness and freedom each year. You can explore the building and read Lincoln's famous speeches. I hope you enjoyed learning more about the Lincoln Memorial!

Lincoln Memorial Facts

On the statue of Lincoln, his left hand forms a fist. The fist stands for Lincoln's strength. His right hand is open and stands for his kindness.

The memorial is as tall as a three-story building. The marble stairs in front of the building lead down to a long pool. The Lincoln statue and the columns appear in lights at night. These lights are reflected by the pool.

During his "I Have a Dream" speech, Martin Luther King Jr. said, "I have a dream that my four little children will one day live in a nation where they will not be judged by the color of their skin but by the content of their character."

The Lincoln Memorial

Glossary

architect — a person who plans what new buildings will look like and decides how the rooms will fit together

Civil War — (1861–1865) the battle between states in the North and South that led to the end of slavery in the United States

column — a tall, narrow structure that supports a building

commissioners — a person in a group that is responsible for a special task

Congress — the group of people in the U.S. government who make laws

dedication — a ceremony that sets apart a building or structure for a special purpose

memorial — something that helps people remember an important person or event

mural — a painting on a wall

platform — a raised, flat surface

slavery — the practice of owning other people called slaves

slaves — people who are owned by other people and are not free

symbol — an object that stands for something else

veterans — people who have served in the armed forces, such as the Army

To Learn More

At the Library

DeGezelle, Terri. *The Lincoln Memorial.* Mankato, Minn.: Capstone Press, 2004.

Nelson, Kristin L. *The Lincoln Memorial.* Minneapolis: Lerner Publishing Co., 2004.

Ruffin, Frances E. *The Lincoln Memorial.* Milwaukee: Weekly Reader Early Learning Library, 2006.

On the Web

FactHound offers a safe, fun way to find Web sites related to this book. All of the sites on FactHound have been researched by our staff.

1. Visit *www.facthound.com*
2. Type in this special code: 1404837183
3. Click on the FETCH IT button.

Your trusty FactHound will fetch the best sites for you!

Index

Look for all of the books in the American Symbols series:

The Bald Eagle
The Bill of Rights
The Great Seal of the United States
The Liberty Bell
The Lincoln Memorial
Our American Flag

Our National Anthem
Our U.S. Capitol
The Pledge of Allegiance
The Statue of Liberty
The U.S. Constitution
The White House